Praise for THE LEADER'S EDGE

"If you are like me and have a vision to be a leader in the industry, but need direction and feedback on common issues that prevent setbacks and costly decisions, there is no better place to be."

— Gerry Bower, TLC Total Lawn Care

"It is tough to tell a bunch of strangers about the things you know you are doing wrong in your own company. And even tougher to ask for help! I learned some important things about listening and that everyone around the table had a lot to offer sharing their successes as well as their mistakes."

— David Wright, Wright Landscape Services

"At my local association meetings we learn good information... but it is a drop in the bucket compared to what I get out of The Leader's Edge."

— John Newman, Classic Landscapes

"It is a fresh set of eyes my company has needed to stay focused, on target, and profitable!"

— Matt Kulp, Showcase Group

"It will help you tremendously in your struggle to becoming a much more successful business owner."

— Noel Ortiz, Great Outdoors Landscaping

"The beauty of The Leaders Edge is that we exchange best practices, learn from each other and increase the profitability of our businesses."

— NATHAN HELDER, JAN GELDERMAN LANDSCAPING

"By putting together owners so different, it is a testament to your experience with proper group dynamics and how they promote results. Thank you for all you contributed to make the meeting a big success."

— CRAIG KOPFMAN, GREEN ACRES LANDSCAPE & DESIGN

"For me this is an opportunity to learn from others' success and mistakes in a non-competitive environment."

— JOHN RENNELS, PRESIDENT, A PLUS LAWN AND LANDSCAPE

"(It helps me) getting together with like-minded individuals who usually need to be very guarded about the business in their own area who can discuss issues with others that are or may have had similar problems. Generating a support group for now and for the future!"

— GRAHAME HUBBARD, PLANT SPECIALISTS

"I believe every business owner would benefit from this program! It was rewarding to be part of your group, and has motivated me to research how we might offer this opportunity to more of our Landscape Ontario community".

— SALLY HARVEY, MANAGER OF EDUCATION, LANDSCAPE ONTARIO

Also by Jeffrey Scott

THE REFERRAL ADVANTAGE

How to increase sales and grow your landscape business by referral

The Referral Advantage shows you 92 ways to ask for, earn, reward, and inspire more referrals.

"Packed with ideas and techniques you need to grow your business. I highly recommend it!"

— J.Landon Reeve, Founder, Chapel Valley Landscape

"Jeffrey is addressing a critical marketing tactic that is neglected too often by too many contractors. This book is worth reading to help any contractor better leverage their relationships"

— Kevin Kehoe, Consultant

"The book is great! I strongly recommend it for entrepreneurs who want to improve their personal relationships with their clients."

— Tom Shotzbarger, General Manager, McFarland Landscape Services

"Your book The Referral Advantage is right on! It has great insight on growing your business through those that you already know."

— Kevin Payne, Tender Care Lawn & Landscape, KS

"What a great resource! This step-by-step guide to obtaining referrals will be a great addition to any business owner's toolbox!"

— Bruce Moore, Sr., CEO, Eastern Land Management

To order your copy of this book, go to the Planet website or the Landscape Management website, or visit www.jeffreyscott.biz

THE LEADER'S EDGE

Join a Peer Group and Grow Your Landscape Business!

JEFFREY SCOTT

Contact Jeffrey Scott: 203 220-8931

www.JeffreyScott.biz

jeff@jeffreyscott.biz

Cover and Interior Design: AuthorSupport.com

Editorial Consulting: iWordsmith.com

Table of Contents

Table of Contents (continued)

INTRODUCTION

A New Approach to Business

You can't get to the next level of growth by doing things the same old way.

Whether you are facing times of challenge or times of growth, you need to step back and assess what is working for you and what is not.

There's an old saying that goes something like this, "Insanity is trying to get a new result by doing the same old thing." I believe this applies to all of us as we deal with today's challenges; we need to be prepared to take a fresh look at our approach to business.

GET THE EDGE

"What got you here, won't get you there."

MARSHALL GOLDSMITH

Business owners tend to fall into one of three categories when it comes to navigating change:

New School, Old School, and No School. This book is for anyone, from *any* school, who is willing to try a new approach in order to grow his or her business.

What is *The Leader's Edge?*

The Leader's Edge is the willingness to step back from what isn't working and do things differently, until you secure the results you are after. In this book, you will learn why gatherings known as *peer group meetings* are among the most important tools for getting and keeping your Leader's Edge.

Isolation is one of the biggest challenges leaders face. As a leader, you cannot share everything that is on your mind. You can only share certain information with managers, and certain information with friends and significant others. You have to learn to create a balance, and maintain boundaries in these relationships. For this reason, you need mentoring relationships that fall outside of the workplace if you are to create the momentum that will allow you to grow your business. Joining a *peer group* is a great way to build and maintain these additional relationships, in order to overcome the problematic isolation of running a business.

There are four main questions to consider when you are thinking of joining a peer group. Your answers to these questions should not focus on short-term gain, but rather on the long-term growth of the business and of your own leadership skills. The four questions are:

1. What is my purpose for joining, and what new results am I looking to create for my business?

2. Will the group offer me enough confidentiality?

3. Will the group create meaningful accountability for me?
4. Will the group have enough staying power to deliver results over time for me?

My experience is that owners and managers who are part of a peer group not only improve their business, but also improve their ability to manage their emotions. They learn to respond more effectively to the challenges of operating a business.

Recently, one of the participants in a peer group told me:

In Their Own Words...

"I completely changed the way I thought about myself and my company. I got a whole new perspective on running this business. I didn't start this company; I took it over in midstream. As a result, I missed out on a whole level of dreaming and brainstorming about where my company could be going in the future. That's a change that I realize now that I need to make. I need to learn how to move back into the 'what could we do' mindset. I was impressed with the energy and passion coming from some of the guys who had smaller companies than I had. It gave me a whole new way of thinking about myself and my business."

A $1 TO $3 MILLION COMPANY

Another shared this:

In Their Own Words...

"It's very obvious after you spend some time with people that you start to figure out what their strengths and weaknesses are, and simultaneously what your own strengths and weaknesses are. That whole process of finding what has worked for other companies and also where they've stumbled, and then comparing that to my own experiences and my own track record—that was very helpful to me. I learned a great deal about myself, and my company, just from spending focused time with these people. This group process is going to be a big part of our success as we move forward, and it's exciting to be a part of it!!"

A $250,000 to $1 million company

These small business owners gained an important edge in running their businesses. You can gain this edge, too, by embracing the purpose, process and payoffs of belonging to a peer group.

CHAPTER ONE

A Short History of Peer Groups

Peer groups have been around for a very long time—some people trace them back before the American Revolutionary War—but confidentiality concerns, political pressures, and other factors often kept their membership, origins, and working habits obscure.

The main concepts incorporated within modern peer groups were first laid out in Napoleon Hill's classic book *Think and Grow Rich,* which was first published in 1937, and updated and revised several times thereafter.

Think and Grow Rich

In the first edition of his book, Hill defined a "mastermind group" as a "coordination of knowledge and effort in a spirit of harmony between two or more people for the attainment of a definite purpose." He coined the term under the influence of his mentor, the industrialist Andrew Carnegie. He refers to a mastermind group as being composed primarily of Carnegie employees, with Carnegie at its head, focused exclusively on the production and sale of steel through Mr. Carnegie's various companies.

In the years since the book was published, the popular definition has changed, and countless self-described mastermind, accountability and peer groups have emerged. Usually, these have been composed of business owners and leaders who are willing to assist and challenge one another as they pursue individual business goals.

Today's mastermind groups tend to be made up of people from different industries, whereas industry-specific peer groups are made up of people from the same industry. (See Chapter Five for more information on the pros and cons of each.)

Peer Groups Become Popular

Industry-specific peer groups were first formalized after World II, in the U.S. auto industry. Auto dealership owners would join groups for strategy, perspective and to get help improving their financial performance. They would help each other spot inefficiencies and financial opportunities. As the auto industry peer group became successful, other industry peer groups sprouted up.

In the 50's, professionals in the swimming pool industry came together to create purchasing power and help each other with their businesses. This version of a peer group is called a *Buying Group*. One such group was Paddock based in California. My grandfather built a successful pool business based on the help he received from Paddock members across the United States.

Trade Associations vs. Peer Groups

Local trade associations, such as Tree, Lawn, Nursery and Landscape Associations, are the main forums for sharing information and ideas. However, they tend to lack a critical element: the opportunity for a completely unguarded and candid exchange of information. In such groups, your competitors may be in the room, and sharing can be counterproductive.

For this reason, peer groups have become a proven method for accelerated learning and business growth. Facilitating industry-specific peer groups in the green industry is my specialty.

In Their Own Words...

Usually when you sit down talking to a bunch of the local guys, you're skirting around things and you're not really delving into it, because you're trying to feel somebody out. Whereas in the peer group, we just laid it all out on the table.

A $1 to $3 milion company

In Their Own Words...

I think the biggest difference was that in the peer group we're going there with our numbers and our books, and laying it out in front of everybody, which you would never do at a local association. (The value of the peer group is) the ability to really delve into it and analyze the financials....and give constructive feedback.

A $250,000 to $1 milion company

CHAPTER TWO

The Benefits of Belonging to a Peer Group

Beyond the main benefit of improved business growth, there are a number of important reasons you should consider joining a peer group.

One reason to join is to solve problems that are hampering both your success and feeling of success.

Another reason is to increase the confidence and enjoyment with which you manage and run the business. In addition to these reasons, belonging to a peer group will help you:

Gain control over the business. You may feel consumed or overwhelmed by the business; you may feel that the business is running you and you are not running the business. A peer group can help you to change this.

GET THE EDGE

"To associate with other like-minded people in small, purposeful groups is... a source of profound satisfaction."

ALDOUS HUXLEY

Feel supported and get support. You may feel isolated in the day-to-day development of your business. It doesn't need to be this way.

Reduce the headaches and the unhealthy stress involved with running the business. Business always has its stresses; some are good for you, and others definitely aren't. A peer group will help you identify the bad stresses, help you plan better to avoid them, and react more constructively when they happen.

Find new ways to grow the business. Innovation comes in the form of new ideas, new processes, new solutions, new people management methods, and so on. In a good peer group, you will learn new ways to protect and build the value of the business.

Make faster progress and avoid mistakes where possible. You have the right ideas, but you just need a little push to take action. Other times, you are eager to get going, but you can't foresee all the sharp turns in the road ahead. Your peer group should help you in both situations.

Get honest feedback on your leadership and management style. Most people you know are too close to you to give you direct, honest feedback on the most critical issues. A good peer group, however, is designed to do just that.

In Their Own Words...

A big "aha" for me, was getting feedback on the importance of interacting with my employees. I've always been a very strict boss, I guess, where I haven't really considered my employees personal feelings enough, and some of the guys in the group called me out on that and said that I need to show a bit more of a personable side to them, and engage them as well. I went back to my business and did this, and it had immediate benefits. It was a big "aha" for me.

A $250,000 to $1 million company

Discuss confidential matters without compromising your company's competitive position. Talking out loud about large and small issues helps you move forward with the right decisions. The peer group is a great environment for open discussion on confidential issues.

There is one significant unexpected benefit of being in a peer group.

The Unexpected Benefit

A close friend of mine (I will call him Mark) has been a member of a peer group for almost a decade. This peer group has helped him grow his business from a fine small business to a powerhouse business with a stellar reputation in his

GET THE EDGE

People join a peer group to gain a competitive advantage. They stay for the personal friendships they make!

industry. At one point in Mark's career, he and his wife decided to separate. This was not an easy decision, and it wreaked havoc on his business and personal life.

For a few months, Mark's life was in deep crisis. During this period, he was scheduled to attend his peer group meeting. Because of the major changes he was going through, he thought about skipping that meeting, but eventually decided to make the trip. When he entered the room, all his peers rose and gave him a standing ovation. It was at that point that Mark knew he would pull through.

Mark remarked to me that he had initially joined the group to help him grow his business, but he now realized that he stayed in the group for a completely unexpected reason: the strong bonds of camaraderie, friendship, and mutual support he has formed with the other members.

Q In Their Own Words...

Professionally, I gained from the general desire and passion of the group as a whole to improve their companies from a perspective of an owner and as a company in general. The passion and energy within the group I think it what's going to really help me and push me as we grow.

A $1 TO $3 MILLION COMPANY

CHAPTER THREE

Who Should Join a Peer Group

What makes for a good member in a peer group?

This question is an important one because the membership mix will have a dramatic impact on you and your business. Joining a group with the wrong mix will hold you back from your natural development as a leader.

As Charlie "Tremendous" Jones once said, *"You will be the same person five years from now except for two things: the books you read and the people you meet."*

I've been both a participant and a leader of peer groups for just under a decade, and spent a lot of time thinking about who I would want to surround myself with in order to meet my own goals and grow as a leader. I have found that the following people and traits make for the best membership mix in a peer group.

Discretion—is a fundamental

The people in your group need to keep confidences. When you share personal or confidential information with other members, they shouldn't pass it on to people outside the group. The more confidence you have in the discretion of the group, the more you will be willing to share about yourself and your business, the more the group will be able to help you improve on your management and leadership practices. Moreover, the more you share, the more others will want to share about themselves and their businesses. It is a win-win situation!

The group's level of confidentiality has a lot to do with the group facilitator and the tone that he or she sets for the group. Confidentiality agreements can help in this effort, but in the end they are only as strong as the people who sign them. One bad apple in this area can derail an entire group. It is up to the facilitator, and each member individually, to keep the group towing the line of confidentiality.

Confidentiality promotes sharing, and sharing promotes learning!

Achievement-minded members—help you grow

The best groups are filled with open-minded businesspeople, as opposed to people who already know everything there is to know. An achievement mindset means that you are open to others questioning you, and you are willing to "look under all the rocks" in your business to find new ways to increase productivity. Spending time with these "high achievers" will help you cultivate this mindset in your own life.

The achievement mindset is one of success and optimism. Achievers do not give up on themselves or their peers. Achievers help others succeed. If you join a group, look for those populated with members who share this mindset.

Diversity—expands your thinking

The more diverse the opinions within the group are, the more diverse the insights and perspective you stand to gain. I once ran a group with members from different European countries who spoke different languages. I currently run green-industry groups that have many voices: Southern twangs, city talk, country thoughtfulness, and Midwestern steadiness. I have found that diversity will keep a group energized and increase the number of ideas raised and explored.

GET THE EDGE

Diverse experiences and viewpoints will help your group stay energized and grounded.

Diversity in membership creates an innovative environment.

Your peer group members can have different ages, different-sized businesses, and different experiences. All that is fine, as long as they share the achievement mindset.

Good Character—helps you become a better leader

For a group to perform well, your co-members should have your best interests at heart. You want them to be giving you ideas and advice that protect and support your business and your personal and professional reputation. This takes good character and good judgment. Surround yourself with people who will make you a better person and a better leader.

In Their Own Words...

It's amazing to know that it doesn't matter geographically where you're located or even what type of business you have in the green industry. Business practices and principals—whether they be HR, financial, sales—still remain the same. It was neat seeing that in different companies from different areas.

A $3 to $10 million business

Competitors—do not make good members

There are two types of competitors: companies that compete directly (same service, same customer) and companies that compete indirectly (different service, same customer).

If the group you are considering features someone who serves the same customers you do, and you feel even the slightest twinge of misgiving, you should find another group.

In Their Own Words...

"The great thing about these meetings is that you get past the problem of being a potential competitor with the person you're asking advice from. In your own geographical area, you see people who are direct or indirect competitors, and generally speaking, everybody will tend to be tight-lipped about information that matters. That isn't the case with the peer group. You're in a safe group, and it's easier for people to start opening up. That's what really drives the value through the roof (for me)."

A $250,000 to $1 million company

CHAPTER FOUR

The What, When, Where, and How of Peer Groups

People who are unfamiliar with peer groups are often curious about how they work. In this chapter, you will get a quick overview of the *what, when, where,* and *how* of peer groups.

How many: The goal of a group is to create an environment that allows members to help and support each other to achieve their best. Groups can accomplish this with between 5 and 20 members; the sweet spot is between 8 and 12 members.

When: Groups tend to get together on a monthly, quarterly or twice-yearly basis. More important than how much time you spend *in* the peer group is how much time you spend preparing *for* it. One of the critical indicators for a group's success is the willingness of each individual member to invest time between meetings following through on action items from the last session, preparing for the next session, and helping out other members.

GET THE EDGE

No matter how good you are at running your business, you will benefit from the increased accountability, energy and perspective that a peer group creates.

Where: Meetings can take place in any number of different venues such as: hotel conference rooms, library rooms, country clubs, vacation resorts, or the company facilities of a member of the group. I find great value when a group can meet on-site at a member's facility. The reason for this is simple: You learn so much more when you can speak to key personnel, walk through a member's facility, and even see where a member has his or her office in relation to the company's staff.

Meetings can also take place on the phone or over the Internet. Phone and video calls are great for maintaining accountability, staying informed, and getting quick help on new burning issues.

In addition, each member of the peer group should have the opportunity to meet and/or talk by phone with other members one-on-one. These ad hoc and preplanned conversations help members keep momentum going on the execution of their action plans, and also help people bond with each other and stay in touch.

In Their Own Words...

Professionally, it was good to visit and be immersed in their facilities. I find that at other group meetings I've done at a hotel conference room, you don't get a sense of the company. (Here) you get to meet some of the key management team and you get to question them in a very confidential setting, and hear how they think and see how they work. I thought that was extremely helpful.

A $1 to $3 million company

How Much: Membership fees can range from free (for self-formed mastermind groups) to upwards of "five figures" for groups that meet extremely often.

How Members Learn: The ultimate goal of a peer group is learning and improving. Learning happens when:

You are on the hot seat explaining and exploring an issue, obstacle or opportunity in your business.

You are sharing insights and experiences with the group while someone else is on the hot seat.

You are listening to conversations between others and gaining new insights on the thought process someone else is using to solve a problem.

You are listening to an employee (of a member) being interviewed about their job, their company and their competition. You might be surprised at the "aha" moments that happen when you get to talk very openly and honestly with a key employee at another company.

You are listening as case studies are presented—the good, the bad and the ugly. Or you are presenting your own case study and getting feedback from the group.

You are participating as successful processes are shared between members.

You are processing what you have heard and creating your own action plan for your company.

Learning happens throughout the peer group process; by being present, by sharing, and by listening and adapting to your business what you hear being shared and discussed by the group.

CHAPTER FIVE

Two Types of Accountability Groups

There are basically two types of accountability groups you can choose from.

1. An "industry peer" group, made up of people from your industry, usually located in different towns and states.

2. A "mastermind" group, made up of people from different industries, who share something else in common, e.g., they come from the same town.

Some people hear the phrase (industry) peer group, and immediately assume that it is identical with the concept mastermind group. As I mentioned in Chapter One, these two kinds of gatherings are different, and each presents both advantages and disadvantages. This chapter compares and contrasts the two groups.

PROS of Joining a (local) Mastermind Group Include ...

The people you meet there are likely to have a good understanding of the local business environment.

Attending the meetings will build up your local referral network.

Your contacts may have a decent understanding of state and local regulations.

Meetings can be scheduled more frequently.

Joining the group may be free (though some can cost over five figures annually).

CONS of Joining a (local) Mastermind Group Include ...

The people in it are probably not operating in your industry.

You can't benchmark your company's performance against the performance of other companies.

You may not be sharing sensitive financial information; and even when you do, you may not be comparing "apples to apples."

You may not have the same personnel, systems and financial issues as the other people in the group.

You do not do in-depth facility tours.

The members of the group can't confidently challenge you on industry-specific issues.

PROS of Joining an Industry Peer Group Include ...

There's usually a fee to join (which means each participant is committed to the process and to one another).

Industry issues are taken seriously.

If you go on facility tours, you get more out of them.

You receive both leadership and operations help.

Participants understand intuitively what each member is facing in the day-to-day operations of each business.

Participants generally share similar business processes.

Assuming that the membership is chosen to exclude direct competitors, participants are extremely comfortable sharing their own sensitive financial information and ratios with the group.

In Their Own Words...

I found that the on-site company evaluation was extremely valuable. To be able to go to another company and critique their business like that professionally, together with a group of guys in the same business—it brought out a lot of other looks at issues that I might not have thought about before. It was worth its weight in gold.

A $250,000 TO $1 MILLION COMPANY

CONS of Joining an Industry Peer Group Include ...

There may be more travel (which is a negative only for those who dislike travel).

The groups tend to meet less often than mastermind groups, but they usually meet for longer time periods, and go much more in-depth when they do meet. I find this to be a positive.

CHAPTER SIX

Peer Groups Make Your Best Board of Advisors

A competent board of advisors can give you a significant competitive advantage, whether you are experiencing economic challenge or strong growth.

Many high-growth companies, regardless of the industries in which they operate, have a board of experienced advisors who offer management insights, guidance and accountability.

Your company can enjoy the same advantage; and participating in a peer group is probably the easiest and quickest way to do so.

Taking part in an established, industry-specific peer group will help you avoid the common pitfalls that traditional boards of advisors can experience. These common pitfalls include:

- Avoiding the tough questions, because board members don't want to offend the owner, who may be a friend or a client of theirs.
- Having conflicts of interest. For instance, board members may work for the company in some capacity (as an accountant or consultant) and they don't want to "bite the hand that feeds them".
- Not doing their homework between meetings. I have seen this happen many times. Board members don't realize that showing up is simply not enough.
- Not knowing how to fulfill their role—they generally don't get training on how to become an effective board member.
- Not having proven business experience.
- Lacking diversity. Boards are sometimes made up of friends and buddies of the owner, and thus, the advice given tends to be less powerful than it could be.
- Not understanding your business. For example, their experience may be limited to the white-collar sector, or they may not have an understanding of your equipment, regulatory and seasonality issues.

On the other hand, industry-specific peer groups, when expertly facilitated, give your business the very best chance for success. The following are some of the reasons that a peer group can become your best board of advisors:

Improved financials: The peer review process will help you read, understand, and more effectively critique your financials. In a peer group, everyone gets better at reading the financials.

GET THE EDGE

"We made too many wrong mistakes."

YOGI BERRA

Up to speed quickly: You'll get good advice much more quickly than you would from a traditional board of advisors. In an industry peer group, you can get down to business right away, because there's very little learning curve for peers. A traditional board of advisors can take twelve months or even longer for new members to get up to speed.

In Their Own Words...

"The openness (at our first meeting) was a pleasant surprise. I expected that it would have taken longer for that type of situation to develop and it didn't. It took only two or three hours and everyone was behaving in a very open manner. We all felt free to share quite sensitive information."

A $250,000 TO $1 MILLION COMPANY

Make better decisions: The members of a good industry peer group are not easily fooled or misled. They know what it's like to run a business in your industry, and they can draw on decades of combined industry-specific experience to generate wise, creative recommendations.

Committed membership: The members of a good peer group are mutually committed to each other's success. You will find that the more they help you, the more you will want to help them.

Get full value: You can immerse yourself as a participant and get full value, because you won't be busy facilitating the meeting and you won't have to manage the group outside the meetings. Chances are you may not have the specific skills needed to set up, support, and run a board of advisors. A well-run peer group, by contrast, is all set up and ready to go.

Help between the meetings: Peer group members will be there for you between meetings, and will be up to speed in terms of what is going on within your industry. On a traditional board, the members may be hard to reach and out of touch. They may be off doing their own thing and not thinking about your issues.

A traditional board can be helpful, but a peer group makes your best board of advisors.

CHAPTER SEVEN

Peer Groups Offer Structured Accountability

Michael Gerber, author of *The E-Myth,* advised us to work "on" our business rather than "in" it.

These few wise words capture the challenge of entrepreneurship. Like most good advice, Gerber outlines something that is much easier said than done. Even when you identify the specific areas where you should be working "on" your business, you still face the challenge of finding the time needed to do this work.

As business owners and leaders, we find ourselves responsible for a great many things. Inevitably, some items that ought to get done just don't get done. We get caught up in the day-to-day struggle and minutiae. That's where the value of an accountability group comes in.

> **GET THE EDGE**
>
> *Often you know what needs to get done—you just need to set your priorities and make the time.*

An accountability group is a group of caring and competent business people who help you set priorities with your own time, and help you understand what is important to get accomplished in your business. An accountability group helps you work "on" the most important aspects of the business.

Structured, Meaningful Accountability

Group dynamics play an important role in the success of an accountability (i.e. peer) group. Because no one wants to disappoint the group, each member tends to follow through on his or her stated commitment to the group.

Group dynamics, however, is not enough to guarantee success. Success is more likely to happen when you get structured, meaningful accountability from your group. This is created through a series of steps aimed at uncovering the most important needs and the most relevant solutions. These steps include:

1. Reviewing your financials.
2. Pulling out the underlying issues from your financials.
3. Identifying possible solutions to your issues and then setting priorities.

4. Creating action steps that address your priorities.

5. Being held accountable to your commitments.

Note that accountability shows up as the last point on the list. The "therefore" here is that a structured process helps to create meaningful accountability.

GET THE EDGE

A peer group will help you do the right things (set priorities) and do things right (execute your action steps).

This process works, because the group accountability is reinforced with two other types of accountability, namely:

Accountability from the facilitator who is running the discussion

One-on-one conversations you have with members between meetings

One peer group member shared with me how group accountability had fostered clarity in his thinking:

In Their Own Words...

"Being in the group has made me think about building a more focused company. After one of the peer meetings, I sat down and started talking with my managers about the company's focus. They all sat there and asked me, 'Well, what is your vision?' And that's when I realized that I really haven't been sharing it with them. I wasn't laying it out for them, and that's what prompted the process we're going through right now. I really feel that by being a member of the group, I've been able to focus more clearly on the issues and goals around my vision for my company, on how I'm going to get there, and on how I can share that with my employees and get them energized in pushing it forward. And once we have a common goal and a common vision, that trickles down to the bottom line."

A $1 TO $3 MILLION COMPANY

Litmus Test—to ensure your accountability group is working

Do you leave your group meeting with an actionable plan for addressing a specific problem area in your business? (YES/NO)

Do the other members approve of your plan? In other words, have their experiences proven the direction you are taking is the logical one? (YES/NO)

Are you personally committed to implementing your plan? Are you excited to follow through on your plan, and can you see clearly how your plan will bring you to the goal you are seeking? (YES/NO)

Are your peers committed to helping you attain success? (YES/NO)

Are you prepared to follow up with your group about the status of your plan once you begin implementation? (YES/NO)

If you can answer *YES* to these questions, you know that you are on the right track.

CHAPTER EIGHT

Get The Most Out of "Benchmarking" and "Best Practices"

You probably hear the terms "benchmarking" and "best practices" a lot. In this chapter we will explore their value and how you can best take advantage of them.

Benchmarking: is the process of comparing your performance metrics with other companies. You can benchmark costs, productivity, quality, ratios, and so on.

Best practice: is a technique, method, process, or activity that is believed to be the most effective of its kind—or at least more effective than the familiar alternatives.

While it is important to make use of these two techniques, they sometimes provide you with numbers and ideas that don't directly apply to your business, or that set the bar too low for your business.

A Caveat about Benchmarks: They can be generalizations, i.e., averages taken from a few companies who volunteered their numbers on an anonymous basis. The act of comparing your company with the standards put forward by these unknown companies can open up as many questions as it answers. For instance:

- What is their service mix?
- How do they define and allocate costs?
- Is the performance level they are citing just a blip, or is it a level they are able to deliver year in and year out?
- Are their market conditions similar to yours?

Unfortunately, you often cannot find the answers to these questions; you are forced to take benchmarks on faith.

The other issue with benchmarks is that they are just an average. I find that companies who set expectations that are "above average" have a much better shot of actually achieving above-average results.

When you expect more from your people, you get more from your people.

Peer groups bring benchmarks into focus: In spite of their flaws, it is still helpful to read and understand common benchmarks, so that you know what is going on in the industry. This is where a peer group can be very helpful. When you sit with a group of owners and operators who are willing to share information openly about their companies, you are able to judge clearly what their benchmarks mean in comparison to yours.

It is OK to compare your company's performance to industry standards—but when you compare your business to the specific businesses in your peer group, you will be able to see the variations from one business to the next, and analyze exactly what those differences mean to your business.

GET THE EDGE

Don't copy others blindly. First understand the operational and financial implications—then apply what makes sense.

So consider benchmarks when setting new goals, but don't use them as absolute guidelines and don't let them limit your expectations of what is possible.

A Caveat about Best Practices: The big problem with the best practices you pick up from the grapevine is that you don't always know their financial and operational ramifications. All you've got is a story. However, when you hear about a best practice from a peer group member, you've got more than just a story to go on.

Peer Groups will help you develop "better" practices. The benefit of sharing best practices in a peer group is that you can match up the "great idea" with actual financials and indicators. You can see just how beneficial the best practices are and how relevant they are to your particular situation. In a peer group you have *proof of concept*, and you also have time to explore the practice. You can do a thorough evaluation on your own terms, and apply the solution that makes the most sense for your business.

Here are a few ways to make use of benchmarking and best practices within a peer group setting.

Example 1: Compare applicability of best practices.

A peer group was exploring the issue: "How should I manage my mechanic and equipment needs?" The group learned that one "$3 to $10 million" member could make more money outsourcing the mechanic's job, while others in the group made more by keeping that job in-house. There was no overarching best practice that could be applied equally to each company. The ensuing discussion gave each member a few tools for analyzing their specific situation and for finding ways to improve their productivity and profitability.

Example 2: Avoid problems that other members experience.

One "$250,000 to $1 million" member shared an issue of streamlining the process and reducing the number of people involved in his bookkeeping and monthly statements. He seemed to have too many people involved in the process, and this was creating problems of inefficiency and inaccuracy. After this discussion, everyone in the group understood how and why they should avoid this problem in their company.

Example 3: Make use of field-tested best practices.

One member, in the "$1 to $3 million" volume range, had developed a comprehensive marketing strategy for differentiating his company in the homeowner association (HOA) market. He shared his approach, including marketing materials, specific tactics he used that worked well, ideas that backfired, and ideas that took a little time to get traction. He told the group how he had repositioned his whole company, based on the success of this one strategy.

Everyone in the group came away with an "aha" moment and a new marketing concept that they could consider applying to their business, even if they don't operate in the HOA market.

In this case, hearing all his mistakes and the ways he addressed them was highly instructive—this could only have happened to this degree in a confidential peer group setting.

Example 4: Drill down on a specific problem.

An owner/operator of a "$250,000 to $1 million" business was experiencing a serious cash-flow challenge. His wife had given him an ultimatum: Get the company profitable... He had assumed that his problem was that his payroll was too high, because he had invested heavily in hiring competent managers in order to set himself up for the growth needed for his company to become more than "just a job." By benchmarking his P&L and balance sheet against those in his peer group, he and the other members were able to determine that his payroll expenses were not completely out of line, but that his accelerated loan repayment was causing problems.

He had borrowed money to buy equipment, and he was paying those loans off faster than he needed to. Apparently, his reluctance to carry debt had made him over-prioritize the loan repayments, and under-prioritize his own take-home pay.

In digging further, the group discovered that he had made these decisions in a vacuum without consulting his accountant or other advisors. He resolved to partner up with his accountant on all major decisions, and make cash-flow decisions that keep both his business and his personal life in balance.

CHAPTER NINE

Control Your Cash Flow and Improve Your Bottom Line

Here's the irony of small business: Many entrepreneurs and managers do not fully understand their financial statements, yet they cannot easily grow their business without this understanding.

Some businesses address this problem by putting an infrastructure of *people, controls and systems* into place to help them with their financials. These successful leaders surround themselves with a mix of bookkeepers, accountants, CFOs, tax advisors, budgeting experts, estimating experts, labor track and job-costing experts, financial planners, and others.

It is not easy or always practical for you to put such a cadre of helpers into place. This is where a peer group can be helpful.

A peer group will give you exposure to a wide range of data, best practices, recommendations and resources—all of which will make it much easier for you to understand and manage your finances.

GET THE EDGE

A facilitated discussion around your finances will make it easier for you to understand them, and therefore, make better decisions.

One member of an industry peer group told me that his participation in the meetings made the job of addressing his company's financial issues less stressful and more enjoyable. (Maybe he was sugarcoating the "enjoyable" part, but it is true that the process can be inspiring, even when the subject of cash flow is not.)

In Their Own Words...

"I've always had a budget, but it's been a budget for the entire year, not a month-to-month budget. Taking part in the peer group helped me master the process of creating a budget on a monthly basis, and nailing down what I was spending and why. There are some things that I do that I had always done, and I was able to step back and start making some important improvements to my processes."

A $250,000 TO $1 MILLION COMPANY

Small businesses tend to make similar mistakes

Entrepreneurs and managers within small businesses tend to make similar mistakes when managing their financials; many of these mistakes can be addressed in the peer group environment. These mistakes include:

- Riding the economic cycles up and down, without working to a proper plan.
- Making large financial decisions in a vacuum, without making proper use of advisors. For example, buying another company or their accounts, without understanding the financial and operational consequences.
- Trying to solve one's problems by cost cutting only, as opposed to implementing more professional sales and marketing techniques. (And vice versa.)
- Not reacting in a quick, thoughtful manner to the changes happening in the business and marketplace, or putting a plan together without vetting it.
- Accepting costs and mark-ups without comparing and contrasting them with others in the industry.
- Working by the accountant's monthly (or quarterly) numbers, as opposed to tracking the appropriate operational numbers weekly and daily. Not working by a "financial dashboard."
- Not paying oneself enough, which may give the false impression that the business is making a larger profit

than it actually is. This in turn causes other problems to go unresolved.

- Confusing expenses with investments. For example, marketing may be an expense but should also be treated as an investment.
- Not sharing the appropriate numbers with your staff; not creating accountability for the numbers within your organization.

GET THE EDGE

Learning to make better financial decisions is the job of every small business manager and leader.

Most of the essential decisions that need to be made in your business can be made more intelligently by educating yourself to your numbers, and by learning how to share these numbers with key staff in your company. A peer group will help you do both.

The peer group process will help you make better, more informed decisions, by giving you deeper insights when it comes to:

- ✓ Identifying the operational issues that are reflected in your financials
- ✓ Identifying techniques for improving cash flow
- ✓ Creating a financing strategy
- ✓ Making strategic plans for your business
- ✓ Open-book management with your staff
- ✓ Increasing your take-home pay

In a successful peer group you will:

Share your financials in a complete and open format. This applies not only to the P&L statement, but also to the balance sheet.

Answer questions about your financials, no matter how well you understand them; and no matter how well or how poorly your company is performing. By discussing them in the group, you will learn how to talk about them more confidently within your own firm, and ultimately, how to make more money by managing them better.

Compare your numbers with everyone in the group. This will give you ideas on where you can improve.

In Their Own Words...

I learned a lot about some of the ratios. I found it interesting explaining a balance sheet to a bunch of guys when I struggle with reading a balance sheet myself. Yet, by explaining it to somebody else, it gave me more clarity as to what to look for. Also, the fact that I was reviewing somebody else's numbers, and when something stuck out, I was like, "Whoa, what's going on here." Going through this process makes me look at my own numbers a bit differently.

A $1 to $3 million company

CHAPTER TEN

Fast-Changing Times Require More "Innovation"

In times of change, a company's best weapon to stay competitive is "innovation." This means getting on the cutting edge of new methods, tools and ideas.

This is not always easy to do, when you work "day in, day out" within the four walls of your company. Belonging to a peer group will help you think outside the box and become more innovative.

Innovation is created when people from different places come together to explore an issue or sets of issues. Innovation happens when ideas are shared and new ideas are created or adopted. The peer group process creates an environment to help each member become more innovative within his or her business.

New and better questions: Innovation tends to happen when people ask new questions. This is a natural outgrowth of coming together in a peer group environment; members are encouraged to ask questions of each other in a non-judgmental fashion.

What do you do to…?

Why do you do that…?

Have you considered…?

How will that help you reach your goals in…?

How else could you do that…?

One of the primary purposes of a peer group is to help members, and the main process for doing this is through a series of questions. The questions are meant to help all the members better understand the issue they are discussing. The questions are also meant to open up the members' perspective on how they view their issue and therefore, how they ultimately tackle their issue.

New questions lead to new thinking, which leads to new techniques and approaches.

GET THE EDGE

"Take the attitude of a student; never be too big to ask questions…to learn something new."

Og Mandino

Example: Better Questions Create Better Solutions.

A "$1 million" member raised the issue of implementing better incentives in his business in order to improve his crew's performance. His peers responded with a series of thoughtful questions that helped this member to look at his issue from a new angle. After a vigorous discussion, the member realized his issue was not one of incentives and motivation; rather it was an issue of not having the right person managing his operations.

> **GET THE EDGE**
>
> *Ask a better question, and you will get a better result.*

He realized he did not have his top people in their right positions in the company. He was asked to do a gap analysis on his three key people in order to identify what their strengths were, and where in the organization they would best fit. This member has since made significant improvements in his business—and he has raised the bar on himself in terms of what he expects from his Operations Manager position.

The unseen advantage: Most members of peer groups I lead tell me how surprised they are at the quality of questions, and thus, the quality of the results that come out of the peer group process.

Innovation is both a habit and a mindset. By asking better questions at work, you will practice the habit of holding yourself and your organization accountable to a higher standard.

Investing your time and energy in the right peer group leads you to a conclusion that many entrepreneurs overlook: It is impossible to improve your business in a meaningful way without opening *yourself* up to developing new ways of managing and leading the business.

In Their Own Words...

It was a huge benefit for me to be able to speak openly about different issues in my company. And then having the other members in the group ask me additional questions on that specific issue without giving me advice, and I really enjoyed that because it made me think deeply and really question what my core issue really was. And as I was explaining the issue to them in more detail, the answers started to fall out just by themselves.

A $3 TO $10 MILLION COMPANY

CHAPTER ELEVEN

Maximizing Your Return on Investment

You will make two investments in your business: time and money.

Once you make the decision to join (or start) a peer group, you need to make sure you maximize your time and money invested in the group.

Free Group?

One way entrepreneurs and managers try to maximize their ROI is by reducing expenses—in this case, by joining a free peer group. While such a group may give you a shot of energy short-term, the long-term value is questionable.

There is an old saying: "You get what you pay for." In fact, you've probably shared these words with a client at some point. The advice you gave to your clients holds just as true in relation to your own development. If you have a strong vision and want to build a business of significance, you will have to invest real dollars and real time in your company's growth and your own growth.

GET THE EDGE

"You get out of a group what you put into a group."

MATT KULP,
PEER GROUP MEMBER

Facilitated Group?

An experienced facilitator will help you put your time to good use while in the group. A good facilitator understands that the more you share and put into the group, the more you will reap from the group. His or her job is to run the meetings so you maximize your return on your time and money invested in the group.

Tradeshow Networking?

You may decide that spending time at seminars and trade shows or simply visiting friendly companies for a day will provide you with the learning that you need. This may be true for start-ups, and for entrepreneurs who are uncomfortable working in a small-group format. For those who want to maximize their time, a small-group format peer group will allow you to tackle your issues in a very time-efficient manner.

Set Up a Board?

We covered this issue in an earlier chapter, but I want to add one more point to the discussion. Regarding costs, a board can be an extremely expensive proposition; you have to pay for each person who sits on your board. Their day rates can add up with quarterly or even annual meetings. Some people will sit on your board for free, but there again, you get what you pay for.

> **GET THE EDGE**
>
> *The quality of the group facilitator will determine the quality of your ROI.*

Hire a Consultant?

You can hire a consultant and pay less (or more) than you would pay for joining a peer group. The advantage is that the consultant gives you a dedicated experience to help you solve a specific problem. The disadvantage with consultants is rooted in the fact that you only get one of them. You do not get a diversity of perspectives and solutions and tools. A peer group will look at your issue from many different and stimulating viewpoints. A consultant has one perspective and one set of ideas.

> **GET THE EDGE**
>
> *Measure your ROI both in terms of financial gain and in terms of your personal growth.*

The other disadvantage is that some consultants are more focused on coming up with ideas, and not on the implementation. All in all, you should look at these as two separate solutions to two different problems. Use a consultant to solve specific, hot issues. Use a peer group to grow your business year over year, and use a peer group to stimulate your growth as a leader.

A peer group should give you a good ROI in both tangible and intangible ways.

Tangible returns.

- Improved bottom-line performance of the business
- Improved cash-flow management; less stress and faster growth
- Improved worth of the business: better systems, improved profitability and balance sheet
- Increased money in your pocket (or invested back in the business)

Intangible returns.

- More consistent creation and implementation of your strategies; less reactive management
- More enjoyment of your business, month-to-month and quarter-to-quarter
- Less stress when issues do arise
- Increased emotional intelligence and improved leadership skills
- More friends in your life (from the peer group); a more interesting and enjoyable learning experience

In Their Own Words...

I've always said 'take care of the pennies and the dollars will take care of themselves.' And that's why I was happy to gain all these ideas – I got 21 ideas that I wrote down from our last meeting. $10 (savings per person) here, $50 there. Not all of them are big, but together they will make a big difference. At the end of the year and especially because of the size company we are, these ideas can relate to thousands in savings. So bottom line, if I implement even the top three ideas, this quarter is going to increase my profitability and increase the personal time with my family. Both of those are good.

A $1 TO $3 MILION COMPANY

CHAPTER TWELVE

Why Peer Groups Fail

Sad but true: Many people who join peer groups do not attain the business improvements they originally sought. Either the group falls apart after a few meetings; or worse, the group meanders from meeting to meeting without adding sufficient value to its members.

Peer groups can fail for any of the following reasons:

- No one is in charge, and people waste time trying to figure out what happens next and how to get the most value from the group. Alternatively, the group becomes a collection of friends who meet but don't challenge each other sufficiently.

- The group is full of local companies, and members are afraid to share confidential information.
- People show up when they want, and take time off when they want. There is no real commitment from group members and the no-shows hold the group back from gaining momentum.
- There is apathy among group members and a lack of interaction between meetings, which can create a lack of energy at the actual meetings. These groups can do OK but they have not maximized the value for each member.
- There are only shallow discussions, where tough issues have been avoided, and the conversations tend to skim along the surface and not address the underlying problems and issues of each member.

GET THE EDGE

When peer groups fail, this is usually due to a lack of a process, or a lack of accountability for implementing the process.

Every facilitator has his or her own facilitation process. I have found and developed a process that works well. (See the Epilogue of this book for a description of it.) If people don't develop a measure of trust with the process the facilitator outlines and executes, or if the facilitator has no process to execute, then failure is virtually certain.

A group with no process, or without a facilitator to implement that process, may seem less expensive at the outset. In fact, such a group always ends up being prohibitively expensive.

In Their Own Words...

I feel like it was a great experience to get together with other business owners in a somewhat casual atmosphere, but to also have some structure there provided by you, and have an agenda and have a format that we followed. It was helpful to have you keep us on track and keep an eye on what the goals were and the outline of the agenda.

A $1 to $3million company

EPILOGUE

Peel the Onion – A Four-Part Process

In the final analysis, a group's success is based in large part on the strength of the process that's driving the group. Here is the process I use;

- **Framing the Issue.** In this first part of the process, I challenge the owner/operator of the business in two ways. First, I may pull him or her aside and discuss the issues they are having, and help the member to frame the issue so the group can effectively get a handle on what the member is looking for. The member then takes the hot seat and describes their pressing business challenge. Issues are best when they are specific, fixable challenges, not generalized complaints that have no target attached to them. (For instance, a good issue might be framed as, "The average dollar size of my projects is not as high as I want," rather than, "The sales team lacks creativity.")

- **Peeling the Onion.** Here, I challenge the group as a whole to explore the issue the owner/operator has just raised. What assumptions are built into the description of the problem we just heard? (Assumptions are always waiting to be found just beneath the surface of any description of any problem.) Also, is there an "issue behind the issue" that we need to uncover and examine? We do our best to refrain from trying to solve the issue right away. Rather, we ask questions to help peel back the layers and expose the underlying issue. Hence I call this, "peeling the onion."

- **Feedback, Benchmarking, and Best Practices.** Here's where the other members get to add their "two cents". What is their closest experience in resolving this problem, or something similar to it? What tactics worked in a measurable way for them? How could those tactics be adapted to this situation? What is their advice and feedback to the member on the hot seat?

- **Accountability.** This is where the rubber meets the road. With support of the group, the "hot seat" member develops an action plan that: a) everyone buys into, and b) the hot seat member is accountable for taking action on. At the next meeting, the owner/operator will be expected to give a status report explaining what has been completed on the action plan, what hasn't yet been completed, and what possible changes in the plan, if any, need to be discussed with the group.

Could this process deliver exceptional results for you and your company? Is *The Leader's Edge* the right peer group for you? Contact me for more information:

Visit: www.GetTheLeadersEdge.com
Call: (203) 220-8931
E-mail: Jeff@JeffreyScott.biz

TAKE THE NEXT STEP

Find out how Jeffrey Scott's *Leader's Edge* peer group can transform your business.

This is a peer program for busy green-industry business owners and leaders, who want to work in a small, confidential group format to grow their business more assuredly and profitably.

To learn more about ***The Leader's Edge*****:**

Visit: www.GetTheLeadersEdge.com
Call: (203) 220-8931
E-mail: Jeff@JeffreyScott.biz

ABOUT THE AUTHOR

Jeffrey Scott has been working in the contracting business since before he could drive. He has done almost every job, from laying sod to digging irrigation trenches, to answering the phones and doing the scheduling, to managing accounting and overseeing sales and marketing.

After graduating college in the U.S., Jeffrey worked for seven years in Europe, where he consulted with companies on how to grow their business, and where he also received a second degree in business. It was in Europe that he first became exposed to the power of the peer groups. He ran groups with members from different countries.

Upon returning to the U.S., he rejoined his family business, and soon was running the design-build-maintenance business, where he doubled sales to $10 million, based on improvements he made with margins, training, client retention and professional referrals.

After taking in the family business experience, he returned to consulting.

Jeffrey now consults in the green industry, helping owners and managers achieve their dreams.

He travels all around North America giving inspirational talks and training at association meetings and within companies. He has spoken from as far away as Holland and Hawaii, in companies from the south and north, and in associations big and small.

He writes columns for the major landscape magazines and for the regional associations, as well as his own newsletter (go to www.jeffreyscott.biz to sign up.)

His passion is facilitating peer groups for green-industry professionals who want to learn new and better ways to run and grow their business.

In his family time, he enjoys traveling with his wife Corine and children (Michael, Max and Kate), mountain biking, golfing with his son, and entertaining friends at home.

To speak with Jeffrey personally call (203) 220-8931 or visit www.JeffreyScott.biz .

Praise for Jeffrey's Consulting, Coaching and Speaking.

"I thought we could improve but I was not sure exactly where. Jeffrey's helped us understand clearly what was working and what needed our attention, and where we could sell more services. Our company is now operationally laser focused on satisfying our target clients, and we have a clearer vision for growth."

— David Bender, Weeded Lawn Service, VA

"The experience I've had using Jeffrey Scott's tools has been very successful."

— Clarke Morantz, Rosedale Landscaping, ON

"Your focus group helped us realize our greatest strengths and has given us direction in how we need to focus the attention of clients to where we are gifted in solving their problems, Thank you Jeff!"

— Leslie Smith, Arborsmith, IL

"I think it's always good to invite outside expert eyes to evaluate what we do and give us feedback. Jeffery understood exactly what I wanted, where I was going and gave me great, practical ideas that enhanced my efforts. Thanks!"

— Susan Cohan, Susan Cohan Gardens

"Very simple philosophies any business in any industry can implement."

— Travis Breininger, Nature's Accents Landscape Services

"The information and insights that Jeffrey extracted from the customer focus group were priceless; it gave us many honest answers to so many unknown questions, and helped us crystallize our direction for the future."

— Jarod Hynson, Earth Turf & Wood, PA

Good solid information. This information is easy to apply to our business. I think receiving information from someone within our industry is great

— J. Peterson, Wheeler Landscaping

"(Jeffrey Scott) gave us valuable insight… time and money well spent!"

— Rick Longnecker, Buds & Blades Landscape Company, WA

Energetic delivery, insightful, informative

— Shawn Sanders, Turf Tenders

Inspiring and informative

— John Pontarelli, Proscape

I learned exactly what Branding is and that we need to learn how to be unique

— Kathy Richardson, Grant and Power

It reinforced my fear that our company of 22 years has lost contact with our customers

—Jeff Howard

"I can attest to a spectacular seminar, that all of my members who were present benefited in many ways, and continue to experience. Thanks so much for all that you do. Best regards!"

— Joe Tinelli, President NYSTLA

Jeff brought focus to the muddle

— Thome Bournce, Ottawa, Canada

Our company has been focused on direct response marketing in the past and only beginning to place an emphasis on branding the company. Jeff provided a really great framework to build our brand

— David Chu, GreenLawn Fertilizing

This seminar really helped me in analyzing where my company is at as far as branding and what we need to do to become more unique

— Jacquelyn Shurbutt

Jeff made me realize I need to spend time with clients getting to know them better in order to stand out

— D. Batey, Ruppert Companies

Jeff gave a good definition of branding and how I can implement and strengthen our brand

— Jerry, Arbor Lawn

After learning about branding from Jeff, my existing clients or any future ones will know exactly why I am the company to fulfill their needs

— **Shannon Ridley, 3D Landscape Group**

Very interesting and enthusiastic speaker. His ideas are practical and useful for companies of any size

— **Teresa Croy**

Your customer survey information was very eye opening

— **Greg Roemer, A to Z Lawn**

It helped create a more clear and concise strategy about branding and our company image

— **Matt Griffin, Prime Lawn**

Jeff gave a new meaning to thinking outside the box

— **Tim Bushman, Suncrest Gardens**

I have been motivated to let customers we've had for years know how much we appreciate them, and I need to check on them in person more frequently. This will get them to talk about us

— **Matt Kruse, Ultra Lawn**

Jeff showed me new innovative ways to keep my customer retention high.

— Kyle Ratcliffe, Dr. Green

Best thing for me today! Get back to basics and show the love. I took over a 25 yr old company that is known for being cheaper and has a lot of older clients. I think I learned everything I needed. It was great!

— Chuck Morgan, Woburn, MA